Always employment & always money in your pocket,
every day

Always employment & always money in your pocket, every day

Jasmin Hajro

Jasmin Hajro

© 2018 Jasmin Hajro

ISBN-13: 978-1722367565

ISBN-10: 1722367563

Cover design by

Jasmin Hajro

First english edition 2018

In this book you'll discover :

The bio of author Jasmin Hajro

&

book Always employment & always money in
your pocket, every day

The bio of author Jasmin Hajro, nice to meet you

Hello dear reader, how are you ?
Thank you for buying my book.

.

My name is Jasmin Hajro,
I was born on July 6, 1985 in Bosnia.
As refugees, we came to the Netherlands 21 years ago.
After having completed school & worked at several jobs ...

On 17 December 2012, I founded my first company:
investment firm Jasko.
After a successful first year, I unfortunately had to close that
company. After a short period of rest, unemployment and
temporary work. I started again as an entrepreneur.

On September 1, 2015, I founded establishment Hajro.

(We say establishment instead of company,
because we do a bit more then just sell stuff.
Like providing jobs,
donating to 40 different charities,
and helping people to live richer.)

Since the beginning the core activity is,
selling sets of greeting cards, door to door.
Nowadays the product range has been expanded.

With, among other things, the selling of my 12 books.

The royalties of my books are donated to the charity:
foundation Giveth Life.
From there more than 40 other charities receive donations.
And by buying this book you support more than 40 charities.
Thank you.

My company is now part of Hajro Group,
which consists of 19 different subsidiaries,
that are part of 1 umbrella organization :
Called Energy Now.

For more information about my company
& the foundation,
go to my website : **www.hajrobv.nl**

Hi dear reader,

how are you ?

I am Jasmin Hajro,

and you just have read a few things in my bio

about me.

I am 32 years old and live in Doetinchem,

in the Netherlands. I work as a salesman

on behalf of Hajro.

I sell sets of greeting cards,

gift mugs and booklets.

A part of the proceeds goes to 40 Charities.

You can find everything about establishment Hajro at

www.hajrobv.nl

But it hasn't been like this always ...

It has been completely different.....

It was 2015 in the evening around 10 o'clock.

I walked outside,

without money,

with my phone that had no credit on it.

It started raining,

The last thing that I needed was rain ...

I did not know where to go ....

I could not call anyone.

I had had some friends,

but I hardly had any contact with them.

I went into a playground in

our neighborhood ....

I had went there also the previous time.

The previous time,

when I was also kicked out of the house & on the streets at night.

My mother couldn't endure our home situation anymore,

she demanded that I give her my house key.

I gave her the key and left ...

She doesn't even own our house, but she pays the rent.

There I was,
homeless,
on the street,
in the rain............

It started to get colder.

I have been able to hide in that playground
in some kind of wooden little house.

I was angry,
when I had cooled down,
I started to think more clearly.
And wondering where I should go
and what I should do?

When it became morning & the sun started to shine
I walked to the center of the city.

Everything was still closed, it was too early.
The church was also closed.

I had heard about some kind of shelter
that a friend of mine had talked about.
He has moved to England some years ago.

So I walked towards the Iris shelter for the homeless.

When I arrived there, I told them my story,
and received a cup of coffee with milk in it
(I never drink milk in my coffee)

But they had no room for me!

So the people who's job is to help people who are homeless,
couldn't help me.

Fuck the so called help.

I could go to day care,
but that was only during the day.
At night I had to sleep outside, on the streets.

On the way to the daycare,
I thought :
I have to go to Arnhem, to Appco.

To sell,
as an energy consultant
you always have work.

At the daycare
I had to pay for a meal.
But I did not have any money at all.
I could get a meal on credit. (Later I should pay for it)

I had to register with the municipality
for a social welfare.

Just went outside to smoke,
made a little talk with a few homeless people,
who were there too.

Went back in again.
There was a telephone for me,
my sister and her at that time boyfriend called.

They were coming to pick me up .....

Finally when we arrived at home, it was time to eat.

I was hungry like a bear.

I was so pissed

that I could not look at my mother.

I looked at the table.

Because I was so angry,

close to hatred ....

So angry.

Mama asked if I had learned something?

We talked..

I apologized.

And I went to bed,

exhausted.

I had not slept all night.

Nobody was there for me that night
they were not standing in line
to help me.

Even the people who help homeless people,
whose work it is to help them.
Could not do anything for me.

Well,
the next time someone says to you
that money is not that important.

Then that someone talks out of his ass
and not out of his mind.
And you need to make that very clear to
that person.

If you do not have money you can not buy food and drinks.
If you don't have money to pay your rent for 3 months,
then you are kicked out on the streets and
you are homeless.
If you don't have money to buy food and beverages for 2 months?
Then you will die from starvation.

I realized that the house we lived in is not mine.
And neither is the garden.
I almost did not have anything.
Except some clothing,
300 books
and some things.

I hated doing chores
in the garden.
Because it is not my garden.

Also, first I put you on the street
and then you can do chores for me.

You're completely out of your mind, I thought.

But because I did not bring any money into the house,
or paid for living expenses,
I could help out by
showing some contribution and doing chores.
Was her reasoning.

Before all that,
before my homeless night on the street.

Was a time when I could not find employment,
except production work (which I never could endure for long)
So I started my own business. A investment firm

Called Jasko.

Because I loved investing
and I could do it too.
I already had experience and invested for myself,
when I had a permanent job as a cook
at Palestra / Landal in Doetinchem.

So I reasoned, I could also invest
professionally for other people.

I had no experience with selling
or with selling myself.

I found 5 customers,
my father, my mother, my sister,
my ex-girlfriend and a friend of my mother.

Plus I invested my own money in the portfolio.

I invested mainly in mutual funds,
to reduce the risk.
And we were invested in many different companies
globally. Thru the mutual funds that we had money in.

There was about 1600 euro's in the portfolio.

It was making very small profits
almost daily. But cents & a whole euro on some days.

I paid the promised 10% return to my clients.

And a bonus return of 2.5%

I donated a modest amount
to a charity,
on behalf of investment firm Jasko.

It was clearly not enough
to make a living.

There should be a 100thousand euro's in it,
so that I could make tens and hundreds euro's as profits.

I started buying options.
I had no experience with that.
Lost some money.

Made some profit.

Lost some more money.

My sister moved in with us again,
after her relationship had ended.
That boy had not been good to her,
she returned home with a lot debt.

So there was not enough money coming in at home for
3 people. Mama's minimum wage
maintained the survival of 3 people.

If there came a bill for the
yearly municipal tax (500 euros per year)
then it could not be paid.

I really believed in my company
and did not want to do anything else.

I had also applied for a patent

for my financial system and

my idea for a investmentfund.

The 2 things that my investment firm was based & founded on.

But I actually had to start looking for other work.

I started with Hajro Klusjes,

to do household chores

or the garden for other people, for a fee.

I started working for an elderly man in our neighborhood

cleaning and vacuuming,

dusting off his house.

Then I also started looking for work

via employment agencies.

Thru their help I started at Rabelink

as a loader / unloader of trucks.

I eventually signed out my company in 2015,
out of the Chamber of Commerce.

I was very sad.
And became a little lifeless.

A kind of social worker wanted me than,
to sign some kind of agreement,
which meant that I would give up control over
my finances and life.

The Bitch
Damned so called help.

I no longer believed in help.

Self help was the best help,
Dad said once.

And it's the only help there is, I think

My little sister had at that time
already 5 years experience with selling.
(She is only 5 years younger,
no small child or something)

She had started a new business with her
new boyfriend and a colleague from the past.

Called : Your advantage now partnership.

She was also founding a foundation with her boyfriend.

Foundation living together with others.
I have seen the founding document,
drawn up by 026notary in Arnhem.

And I got a chance to start selling greeting cards.

Oh yeah,
that loading / unloading job
has gone like all other jobs,
that I did not want to do.
I showed up a few times too late for the job,
and eventually I did not show up at all.

Selling greeting cards,
would be a good workout
to eventually become an energy consultant
going door to door.

The sales process is the same.
Speak to 100 people a day,
make 3 laps so you speak to everyone
in your terry (work area)
The pitch (your presentation)
is the same with every person who
you speak to.
And so on.

I got training from them,
Emina my sister and her boyfriend.
I also started looking at seminars
about sales (selling)
on Youtube.

Practising my pitch.

I started to become enthusiastic.

I was at home one day
looking at those greeting cards.
And I thought to myself,
I can do what they do.

And anyway what's the worst that can happen,
if I forget the pitch,
or start stumbling my words.

Emina said the worst thing that she got was
a doorslam.
When someone closes the door with a slam in front of you.
Ha, just that?

So I took my pitch on a note,
a money bag and a number of sets of greeting cards.

And began to walk and sell,
I just started in my residential street ...

Before I was ready for it.

I sold a number of sets,
the people were much nicer than I had expected.

I think many people want to do something good.
Even if it's only buying a set of greeting cards
for charity.

The foundation is allowed give rewards to her
management and employees.

The website of the foundation did not work.
Emina and her boyfriend split up.
He had the bill for the founding document
of the foundation, never paid.
The foundation was not yet technically founded.

To get rid of the hassle.
And to be able to continue selling,
what I started to like in the meantime.

I have with the saved money
from my greeting cards sales
set up my own foundation.
Where everything was alright.
And that is of course:
foundation Giveth Life

Made a website for it,
and I continued to sell happily.

Then the police came a number of times,
because they felt that I was collecting.

I was pedaling,
in my head collecting is:
going door to door with a money bus asking for donations,
without giving anything in return.
I sold a product.

They thought differently ....

I had already again registered with the Chamber
of commerce,
to be an independent energy consultant
and to be able to sell.
With company Hajro.

To get rid of that unnecessary hassle with the
police.
I decided to sell greeting cards,
on behalf of my company Hajro

And to donate part of my proceeds to Charity.

The probability was that in the future the greeting cards demand
would be less,
because of Facebook, Whatsapp
digital cards etc.

So I had to come up with something else,
that people would always use,
but of which would fit about 10 units in my bag
to take with me.

I came up with the handy set ...

A handy set is : A mug filled with candy,
plus a teaspoon, a lighter and a pen.
Wrapped as a present.

Because people will always keep drinking their coffee
or tea from a mug.

I also wanted it bigger
and better. A beautiful store
I wanted to make out of my business.

Eventually it was at
www.hajro.nl

Then someone bought that domain.
Coincidentally. I think there was nothing coincidental about it.

Now I had to create a new website,
the old web address is printed on my
thousands of business cards,
on the flyers,
and even on the covers of my books.

I had to do everything over again.

Well the new and improved website
is of course **www.hajrobv.nl**
and has a fun and unique
E-store.

With only Hajro products.

Of course I love my company Hajro very much.
It's like a baby for me.

We're doing well too,
and support many Charities,
and my books can really help people.
To live happier and richer,
and to make their business more profitable.

I earn my money with sales.

So the royalties (the proceeds)
from my books go to the Charity that I founded.

A good foundation,
called the Giveth Life foundation.
Which has already given families a helping hand.

I would like to tell you more about Hajro,

because it's going to do a lot of good things,

but the intention of this book

is to tell you something else.

Of course you can always

get the e-book Establishment Hajro,

the conglomerate

As a free download

on www.hajrobv.nl, when I finish translating it.

You can go through the E-store

to my authorspotlight at Lulu.

You will automatically get when

you click on one of my books in the E-store (E-winkel),

at www.hajrobv.nl

As you can see,

 since that night when I was homeless on the street.

Since than I always have work and always cash in my pocket,

I now can sell and earn every day of the week.

Thanks to sales (selling)

A blog article of mine:

Salespeople sell something to the market (the people/consumers),
the companies that those salespeople work for make profits.

With a piece of those profits taxes are paid,
the government pays for facilities with that money
that we all sometimes use.
Facilities such as the fire brigade, the police, hospitals,
roads (infrastructure).

Companies are also the ones that donate the most money to
Charities.
And companies also give more money than anyone else,
to the
sponsorship of sports clubs and sports clubs.

And also not unimportant:
companies give millions of people work.

So there is nothing wrong with commerce and
commercial companies.

How can those companies do that ?

Because of sales.

By selling products or services to people,
there will be money (turnover & profit)
that comes in to those companies .
And through sales, money comes in your pockets as well.

" By the way, I started my first company in 2012.
I have made more than 700 sales,
since September 1, 2015 so far.
So I have a track record, and I know what I'm talking about. "

"As you have probably already understood, I earn my money by
selling for my own company. That's my work.

The proceeds from my books go to charity.

I write from experience, I write to help people improve their
personal & business life. "

Well 700 times 5, - euro =
3500 euro
But do not get turned off by that amount ....

For someone who was homeless,
and now has work until his retirement.
Every day work & money in his pockest,
every day.

It is good.

Remember that if you help someone switch
from, for example, his current electric supplier,
to another electric supplier. Which is cheaper for that customer.
You earn 50 euros or dollars in commissions.

As an energy consultant.

And 50 euro/dollar times 700 customers =
35000 euro/dollar

Find 20 people per month,
that you help to switch from energy supplier,
(that means you fill out a form)
and you earn
20 x 50, - = 1000, – euro/dollars a month

With 40 customers per month you earn
2000, - euro/dollars per month.

You only have to find 1 or 2 customers per day.

Do you see what the possibilities are in sales?
Available & possible for you too.

You can start very simple
by selling pens for a euro/dollar .
On Saturday.
1, - euro/dollar per pen.

Then sets of greeting cards.
5, - euros/dollars per set.

Then electric & gas,
to arrange the switch from current supplier to another,
by filling in a form.
And earn 50 euros/dollars per customer.

Then start selling vacuum cleaners or cars
and earn several hundred euros/dollars
per customer.

After that you can start selling houses,
and earn 10,000, - euro/dollar or more
per customer

In sales you have work until you retire!
Job security.

It is best if the company that you are selling for
does some good.
Then you also do something good
and you just feel good about it.
Because you do something more,
than just sell a product or service.

That's why I like to sell for Hajro,
because I support 40 Charities,
and the customers do too.

You can become a volunteer at Hajro,
if you want.
Then you walk on Saturday to sell.
And you get a fee for it.
You learn the trade.
And do good,
by supporting Charities.

Visit us at www.hajrobv.nl

and if you feel good about it.

Please contact us via mail or email.

And otherwise you can always go somewhere else

to start in sales, in the place where you live.

Or you can start your own webshop.

If you want to sell for Hajro .....

Then you will be trained by the same person

who has taught me to sell. My sister.

Emina Hajro now has 8 years of experience with

selling (sales)

She has a track record.

She had an office with 20
selespeople.
She has trained dozens of people
to become a salesperson.

And she has made thousands of sales.

She is the owner of Energy Now (EnergieNu),
that is the overarching organization
for Hajro and Hajro Group.

You can find it on www.energienu.nl

Selling is a very important profession.
As you have understood from my Blog article
the economy moves
thanks to salespeople.

Government employees are also paid,
through the tax on profits from companies.

You can be proud if you become a salesperson
or already are one.

Well, I have told you
how sales literally saved my life.

That I have work until my retirement
and after that if I want.

I showed you the possibilities,
what the salesprofession has for you,
if you eventually grow to sell more expensive products and
services.
Or become a broker =
seller of houses and business premises.

You understand that with my company Hajro,
what is Hajro Group nowadays,
other people
get the same opportunity.
As the wonderful opportunity that I got

Yes, I have by now already 3 times
applied for various wellfares.
All have been rejected.
I can not count on the municipality or the UWV
(organisation for wellfare for unemployed).

But I can count on myself and on selling !
Every day.

I have from Monday, September 18, 2017 to
Wednesday, September 27, 2017,
been selling 10 days running in a row,
and made 22 sales in total.

So every day I made sales & every day I made profits.

Earning money every day.

You can do that too.

Hopefully I have been able to enthuse you
about the selling profession.
And hopefully you will start selling.
Even if it's just 1 day a week.

Or you send someone you know,
who needs work and money
into the selling profession.

Into Sales, where there is always work.

Give that person a copy of this book,
so it helps him or her
forward.

You have now read

book Always employment & always money in your pocket,

every day

You have been offered work until your retirement.

Job security.

Be willing to do the things,

from the book.

Start small,

step by step.

You can do it.

Would you be so kind
to recommend this book,
to the people that you know ?

So that they also buy a copy,
and improve their lives.

And I will promote it.

Then we will make it a BestSeller together, and do good,
because the proceeds go to the Charity.
To that good foundation,
foundation Giveth Life

Super thanks in advance.

I wish for you the best things in life.

Kind regards,

Jasmin Hajro

Met vriendelijke groeten,

Jasmin Hajro

Hajro
Ottawastraat 19
7007 BC
  Doetinchem,
the Netherlands
KvK : 65686300

www.hajrobv.nl

P.S. If you want to share your experience with my book,

send me a little revieuw or email at

j.hajro@hotmail.com

Thanx.